PIGMANIA

(A Stressful Account)

by
Henry Lyle

COPYRIGHT

Published by DIROD Publishing
Printed by Amazon UK in Great Britain

ISBN 9798362129477
First Edition

DEDICATION

My passion is writing poetry with only an occasional foray into other literary genres. All are dedicated to my late dear wife **Annette**, who during this time in my life, was my sole inspiration and support.

However, special mention needs to be made of my children **Constance, Richard, Randolph, Raymond** and **Quentin**, some of whom were regrettably denied my attention and presence during their important formative years.

ACKNOWLEDGEMENT

I am most grateful to **Roddy McDowell**, who has taken it upon himself to collate my extensive collection of writings in such a way that they are now in print so that others may enjoy reading them as much as I had penning them.

Without his help and enthusiasm they would undoubtedly have remained gathering dust in some obscure, forgotten folder, never to ever glimpse the light of day…

EPIGRAPH

It's better to have tried and failed than to live life wondering what would've happened if I had tried…
~ Alfred Lord Tennyson.

*

Better tae hae tried an' failed than ne'er tae hae tried at aw…
~ The Author.

BOOKS WRITTEN BY THIS AUTHOR

THE POET'S CHOICE (Book 1)

THE POET'S CHOICE (Book 2)

SCOTTISH POETRY (Book 1)

SCOTTISH POETRY (Book 2)

NOSTALGIC POETRY (Book 1)

NOSTALGIC POETRY (Book 2)

A MAN AND HIS DOGS

BEVERLEY BROWN

CHAPTER ONE
(The Dream)

I suppose we all have dreams, some impossible while others may just be within our grasp. My dream was always to be a farmer, not a gentlemanly agribusinessman, but a hands-on-grafting farmer on marginal ground or even a smallholder. I had my name on the waiting list for a Department of Agriculture small holding but soon after I had applied, the 'big is beautiful' culture dawned and it was decreed that small holdings were no longer viable and thus no longer supportable by the Department.

Any which did become vacant were sold off to wealthy commuters with a title which forbad their continued use for agricultural purposes; that is to say they were to become pretty little country dwellings set in large gardens. Most of the ground was offered to the neighbouring smallholders who were still working their holdings and they were allowed to purchase theirs at sitting tenants rights. As each one retired they sold off the ground to neighbouring large farmers and put the proceeds into their retirement pots. The result was that productive, vibrant communities of country folks were transformed into ranch style communes inhabited by an urban workforce of pseudo countrymen.

These changes seemed to bring the curtain down on my chances of ever getting into agriculture on my own, thus putting paid to my life-long dream. The four years I had spent working in agriculture in my late teens had left an insatiable desire to 'go it alone' in farming, but with no money or farming connections, that desire appeared doomed to failure. But as most people acknowledge, if there is a compelling urge to do something it rarely diminishes and that's definitely the case with my wish to farm in my own right, even in the most modest way possible.

Throughout the ten years I spent working in Edinburgh as a police officer, I never missed an opportunity to get out into the countryside by attending numerous agricultural shows, avidly reading magazines on country matters and keeping in close touch with friends who worked the land.

During this time, I considered the idea of transferring to a rural police force in order to be on hand if any opportunity to fulfil my dream should pass my way and when offered the post of constable, with a provided police house, my family and I sold up and made the move to East Lothian.

Accepting tied accommodation was intended to only be a short term solution with the intention of purchasing at leisure in our new neighbourhood. Unfortunately, the timing coincided with a dramatic rise in property prices and the meagre sum of £2,764 banked for the sale of our house, quickly paled into insignificance as a viable deposit towards another, especially in desirable East Lothian.

Compounding the problem was the fact that our family was steadily increasing in size, already three children and no plans to call it a day in that respect. Not much hope of us being able to increase our down payment, therefor it looked like being tied accommodation for the foreseeable future. But looking on the more positive side, that left us £2,764 available for investment purposes, a modest sum even in those days, but could it just be the opportunity I needed to get onto the first rung of the agricultural ladder?

My duties as a rural beat officer enabled me to pry into every isolated corner of the County... and pry I did. Every farmstead, large and small was duly visited in the course of my first few months of my service at Haddington. Any farm buildings, irrespective of condition, which appeared to be disused was examined and the owner traced with a view to ascertaining their plans for the property. My earlier employment in agriculture in the area and rural socialising, meant that I was already well known to many of the farming community. This not only opened doors vis-a-vis my search but made me more readily accepted regarding my official duties.

For a while my enquiries regarding property bore no fruit until on day I came upon the little steading of **West Latch** nestling in the foothills of the Lammermuirs, about ten miles from Haddington. It was a pretty little collection of buildings with a small copse of conifer trees shielding it from the adjacent unclassified road. Although being a mile and a half in either direction from the nearest 'C' class road, it had mains electricity, a private water supply and was divorced from the main dwelling house of the same name, which was situated on the other side of the road.

It did not appear to be in use and I learned that it was no longer owned by the occupants of the house opposite. My enquiries revealed that it was in fact owned by **Stuart King of Wolfstar and Easter Pencaitland Farms**, a gentleman in the truest sense of the word and one with whom I was acquainted. Could this perhaps be my chance, I wondered?

With my imagination running wild, I considered to what use I would put the steading and immediately realised that it would be ideal for the rearing of pigs, a responsibility for which I was well qualified having helped establish the little unit on **Spilmersford Mains Farm** a decade earlier.

That evening I telephoned Stuart King and asked if we could meet on a business matter? How grand that sounds, but true to character, Stuart did not put me down and invited me to call at his home the following evening.

The next day my duties took me close to **West Latch** and I spent a few thrilling moments walking through the pig shed, examining the little byre, the hay shed and the small wooden floored grain store. If I could buy it, I knew that with hard work I could make a success of it! (However, little did I know that I would indeed work very, very hard but in the end success was not to be... but that is with the benefit of hindsight.) At that moment, as I stood in the steading, failure was inconceivable and not remotely on my radar.

I spruced myself up that evening and went to see Stuart at the appointed time. (He was a gem of a man who tragically died suddenly in his prime several years later.)

That evening however, he greeted me with a smile which lit up his face and the whole world around him.

"What's this business matter then Harry that you wish to discuss with me?"

"I'm desperate to get into farming Stuart, even in the smallest of ways," I blurted out, "and I see that you have a wee steading at **West Latch** that you don't appear to be using. I think that it would make an ideal piggery and that's what I hope to do… breed pigs. I looked after pigs at **Spilmersford** and would love to set up on my own. I have been looking into it and have done some calculations and think that it would be a viable enterprise."

I talked without pausing for breath in the hope that if Stuart could not get a word in, he would be forced at least to hear me out.

He started to laugh… was my idea so laughable? However, I need not have worried, that was not Stuart's way.

"It's true that I don't use the steading," he replied, "I really just bought it for the ground that went with it for permanent grazing for some of my cattle, so I suppose I could consider selling the buildings."

I could hardly believe my ears. I had been prepared for a negative reaction with some words of consolation and was quite overcome by his willingness to consider my proposal.

"How much do you want for it then, Stuart," I enquired in my best businessman's voice?

"Oh, I'll get someone independent to put a value on it… but don't worry, I won't sting you."

That response from anyone else would have sounded hollow, but I trusted him to keep his word and assured him that I had some ready capital (not a lot) and that I would prepare a business plan to take to the local bank manager to secure overdraft facilities.

I had all the jargon together with the confidence of youth and in my present excruciatingly introvert state, I wonder how I ever managed to carry it off... but I did.

I bought several books on pig farming, including **'Practical Pig Production'** by Keith Thornton; **'Pig Housing'** by David Sainsbury; **'Pig Farmer's Veterinary Book'** by Norman Barron, M.R.C.V.S, Ph.D and **'Pig Farming'** by John Luscomb. I studied them avidly, marrying up their expert advice with my previous experiences at Spilmersford Mains Farm. I did my calculations knowing the cost of breeding stock, the cost of pig food, gestation periods and the expected conversion rate of the modern pig (that is how much body weight they could be expected to gain for a given weight of food). I also studied the current store and dead meat market prices, including set up costs such as tools, building materials, barrows, feeders, farrowing crates and bank interest rates, etc.

With all this information, I prepared a five year business plan broadsheet and on these calculations, I expected to be firmly in the black well within that timescale. I had one great advantage in that I did not have to include labour costs as I intended to do it all myself, while living off my earnings as a police constable. The only unknown at this stage was the actual cost of the property, which I hoped would be covered by my available capital and so eagerly awaited the outcome from Stuart King.

About two weeks later it arrived... he would accept £3,000 for the steading including an acre of surrounding land and to say I was ecstatic would be a gross understatement. It meant my costings did not have to be appreciably altered and I could approach the bank manager safe in the knowledge that my credit and debit lines should converge in about two years time, after which I should get into a modest profit situation. That just left the joust with the bank to be faced...

CHAPTER TWO

(Setting Up)

Bank managers were held in great esteem in those days, as were head teachers, doctors, lawyers and clergy. With a greater degree of autonomy locally they tended to be large fish in small ponds who definitely punched above their weight, so to speak.

In mounting trepidation, I made the requisite appointment with a clerical subordinate and arrived at the bank exactly on time, clutching a briefcase stuffed full of relevant papers and copies of authorities to back up my five year plan. The weel kent cashier ushered me into an oak panelled room where behind a massive desk sat the rather diminutive figure of the branch manager. What he lacked in stature however was amply compensated for by his aura of importance and substance.

"Please take a seat Mr Lyle and we'll have a wee chat about the business proposal you have in mind," he said, pointing to a considerably less regal chair which was placed at the proletariate side of the great desk. I felt like a subject of the inquisition, however his cosy approach and friendly smile helped quell the metaphoric butterflies which were fluttering in my stomach.

I apprised him orally of the situation as it stood and what I had in mind for the future. Having made my pitch, I withdrew my trump card from my borrowed briefcase, handed him my papers and then sat back in sweaty silence as he donned his rimless spectacles and studied the result of many, many hours of blood, sweat and toil, figures, percentages, averages and graphs not being my forte. I had typed them all as neatly as my limited secretarial skills permitted, hoping that utter clarity would work to my advantage. I watched his face as he read the volume of print but his expression never varied as he took in the details and I had no idea whether he was impressed or not. After what seemed like an age, he looked up and smiled,

"You have certainly done your homework Mr Lyle, I'll grant you that."

An ambiguous statement if ever there was one... did he mean that he was impressed enough to back me or simply impressed with the effort I had put into it, meaning thanks but no thanks? Prolonging my agony further, he flicked through the papers once more and then said with a smile,

"I'm prepared to grant you overdraft facilities but restricting them to the amount which you are prepared to commit yourself, namely £3,000. I would not have been inclined to do so had you not been willing to risk all of your savings. The fact that you have an independent income to rely on has also been heavily in your favour... but, having said all that, your costings are extremely detailed and realistic and I can see no reason why business success should not be achievable within two years."

I can tell you that I was a happy boy to hear that endorsement coming from such a secure source. To have the backing of the bank manager was really something in those days as they were not renowned for taking chances. With hindsight, he was not taking any risk at all. By restricting the overdraft to the capital value of my premises which he held as collateral security, he could not lose. However, at the time my mind was not bogged down in the semantics of the banking industry. I now had the green light to go ahead with my farming project and that was good enough for me. I was now in a position to tell Stuart that I wished to purchase **West Latch Pig Farm** and instruct a lawyer to arrange the transaction.

I rushed home to tell my dear wife Annette and in my unbridled excitement and enthusiasm I brushed aside any niggling doubts she raised as merely a wife's natural caution. I was about to become a smallholder at long last and was on my way to fulfilling my dream. The fact that there was no house with the property and that I would have to make a daily round trip of some twenty miles, seven days a week, fifty-two weeks of the year in sickness or health left me undaunted. I tremble now at the thought of that undertaking but it is alarming the risks I was prepared to take in blind ambition and naivety. I had convinced myself that I could take it all in my stride with youth and reckless energy on my side.

That evening I called at **Pencaitland Farm** and informed Stuart that I had secured sufficient working capital and wished to progress with the purchase of **West Latch** as soon as possible. We exchanged details of our respective law firms and shook hands on the deal. However Stuart, true to his character and generous spirit did not subject me to that interminable delay while lawyers in their own meticulous way, dotted all the i's and crossed all the t's. He was sympathetic to my impatience saying,

"No need to wait until those lawyers exchange endless letters and charge us ridiculous fees Harry, as I suppose that you wish to get on with preparing the steading for your pigs? Well, go right ahead, the keys for the couple of doors which are locked are hanging on a nail behind the byre door."

That was exactly what I had hoped to hear but feared would not happen… but Stuart had come up trumps yet again. He poured me a generous dram and we drank to the success of **West Latch Pig Farm** under new ownership. The following day I was off duty and at the proverbial crack of dawn, was at my holding and with pencil and paper in hand busily sketching out my agricultural future.

CHAPTER THREE

(It's all Mine)

West Latch steading was a rather pretty little place. Its entrance was flanked by two small copses of conifer trees with a snaking drive which led into a courtyard surrounded on three sides by farm buildings.

On the right was a garage with connecting door into a wooden floored grain store. A verandah sheltered the south side which consisted of a general store shed, a small byre and utility area for storage, feed preparation and water taps. The third side of the yard consisted of a large corrugated metal hay shed with double doors on its open end and an narrow doorway which allowed access into the utility area.

What I called the utility area was really the hub of the steading, because it also gave access to the main pig building and paddock. It was as I say, the fulcrum where food or bedding could be distributed throughout the steading without the need to venture into the open air… a distinct advantage on cold winter days and nights!

I do not suppose that many people would be over excited at acquiring such a humble collection of buildings, but I was ecstatic as I walked around and ran my hands over the byre stalls, clay troughs and pen gates. I could smell the few bales of straw which were still piled in the hay shed and on stepping through the door, the air was akin to elixir. I had to pinch myself to believe that at long last, I owned a smallholding, no matter how small. All that was missing was the actual livestock, but I could soon remedy that, now that I had somewhere to house them.

"But to work, Harry," I muttered, in order to drag my mind from its state of mental euphoria back to reality and the mountain of work which lay ahead.

The water supply was from a private spring shared by several neighbouring farms, with mine at the end of the line with a resultant supply which was barely sufficient at the best of times. I would need to provide storage tanks and arrange to have the water piped around the steading. The fattening piggery would require to be converted by installing sow and litter rearing pens; the byre converted into a farrowing house, electricity led throughout for heating lamps and a false ceiling erected in the farrowing house.

I guesstimated the conversions would entail building some seventy yards of three feet high brick walls, mixing and laying about four hundred square yards of concrete flooring and the fitting of gates and water bowls, etc., etc. In addition, I would need to buy equipment such as farrowing crates, barrows, heating lamps, brushes, shovels, arrange for a steady supply of meal and last but most definitely not least, purchase my breeding stock of pigs... and all in my spare time!

It was little wonder that my dear darling wife was a trifle sceptical about the outcome of my venture, but I had the blinkered enthusiasm of someone on a mission and a bloody tiring mission it turned out to be.

The main pig building consisted of ten pens, those on the left sloping towards a central passageway, but those on the right hand-side sloped away from the central gangway towards the rear wall where weep holes led out onto an external yard. That arrangement was no good to me as I did not require openings to the outside but wished them to also slope towards the central passageway as the other side.

I decided to block off the exits and reverse the direction of the slope which would entail raising the level at the back of each pen by about two feet. To achieve this, would necessitate knocking down an existing brick lean-to building, barrowing the rubble into the piggery in order to raise the floor level, bricking up the existing exits and then re-laying the concrete floors to the required slope. All that sounded straight forward enough, so I committed the plan to paper.

That building would also require the installation of a brick built creep area, farrowing rails, with water and electricity supplies to each pen. No problem and I committed that to paper too, thinking that these alterations would make the building fit for the purpose and then wandered through to the little byre.

Having no intention of starting a dairy herd as cows were and still are my first love (excluding Annette of course), the byre was earmarked for repurposing as a farrowing house. The necessary alterations would simply entail the installation of a false ceiling, draught-proofing, water and electricity and the fitting of farrowing crates. A complete doddle in comparison to the work for the piggery conversion and thus so, the details were duly committed to paper.

I walked about the steading, caught up in the excitement of the plans I had formulated and imagined the pride I would have in the accomplishment when the steading was ready to receive the first complement of pigs, completely blocking from my mind the exhaustion, mishaps and tears that the proposed workload would bring in the intervening months. But surely that is what we do when our dream appears to be within reach?

It was the beginning of March and I wished to be in full production by the end of the year. This was something I thought I could realistically manage, as I hopped into my car for the ten miles drive home… a journey I was to make daily without a break for the next four years!

Having agreed upon the purchase and secured the necessary finance, I had to brush the mud off my boots and attend to the less agreeable chore at my lawyer's office to legalise the transaction. My late mother, God rest her soul, had spent her working life since the untimely death of my father when I was only three years of age, in the employ of a firm of solicitors in Edinburgh. During her service, because of retirements and amalgamations, the Firm traded as **Wilson & Young; Terris; Wilson & Laird** and then finally **Laird & Laird**. As they had previously acted for me in the purchase of a house in Edinburgh, I therefor saw no reason why they could not do so in this occasion, so dressed in my best bib and tucker, I headed for the big city...

The Firm's premises were situated discreetly in Queen Street, with only a small brass plate to indicate the nature of the business undertaken therein. Mr Laird (junior) was the archetypal lawyer, immaculately conservative of dress, speech and mannerisms. His office was lined with bookshelves bearing huge dusty tomes and he sat on a high backed leather chair behind a massive knee hole desk.

He stood up as I was shown in by his secretary and shook my hand politely, if rather limply. I explained the service I required from him and he accepted my instructions, but I could feel his disquiet at having to discuss the very subject of a piggery, septic tanks, private water supplies and middens... so much so, that I swear that he was eager to wash his fountain pen on my departure! I do not think that he had ever handled a rustic transaction before, however he did agree to handle my affairs but the process took much longer than anticipated. I learned why sometime later, when Stuart informed me that his solicitor, local to the area, had been plagued by ridiculous enquiries emanating from a perplexed Mr Laird, indicating his total ignorance of rural life. However in the end, they managed to sort it out and I became the legal owner of **West Latch Pig Farm**.

I could now, at long last, get down to the serious business of preparing my precious little holding. At the time I was a regular beat constable stationed in Haddington and working a three shift system of 7am-3pm, 3pm-11pm and 11pm-7am with a couple of days off duty after each period of seven working days. This may sound somewhat onerous, but in one way working shifts was a boon because I had daylight hours available for my holding, providing that I was willing to sacrifice sleeping time, family time and all recreation!

I bought an old car trailer from a local man for the princely sum of £10 and set about collecting all the materials and equipment I required for the project. It was quite a long trailer, some eight feet by four, but the wheels were located right at the back, hence putting all the weight on the car drawbar... hard on the car and almost impossible to manhandle when unhitched. However it was a trailer and I put it to very good use.

A local piggery at **Clerkington** had recently gone out of business and I bought anything which was moveable — farrowing crates, troughs, metal gates, corrugated sheets, etcetera and conveyed them to my holding. I obtained bricks, sand, cable and piping from a builder's merchant and bags and bags of cement direct from a local cement works. Having assembled everything which I thought that I would possibly need, I set about the mammoth task of singlehandedly converting my little steading into a viable pig farm.

CHAPTER FOUR

(The Work Begins)

I would like to put on record at this point, my appreciation of the sacrifice made by my (now late) wife **Annette** who, devoid of support, was caring for our three children under the age of seven, while heavily pregnant with our fourth. I am the first to concede that I was not alone in working all the hours that God sent.

I had no mechanical assistance by way of powered cement mixer or trolly, so I mixed by hand, barrowed ton upon ton of rubble, cement, sand and concrete as well as the arduous work of actually building walls, spreading concrete and installing piping.

Occasionally I came across a real find... the local auctioneers, **Lesley & Lesley** had accumulated a pile of old bed irons, the angle runners on which the old spring bed bases rested upon and were only too pleased to sell them to me for a nominal sum in order to clear floor space in their premises. After the corner pieces were sawn off, they made ideal channels for the brick work to bridge the creep areas. However, I digress and must confess that not all my purchases were as successful.

Looking back, the hours of work which I put in was akin to pure slavery, but at the same time, accepted that to succeed in business, you should be prepared to work hard and that is what I did. I would ordinarily finish a day shift at 3pm, drive directly to the holding and work there until about 7 o'clock, arriving home just in time to see the children before they went to bed.

Annette would re-heat my dinner only to be rewarded by me falling asleep as soon as I sat by the fire.

On a back shift, I would be at the steading by 8am, carrying a packed lunch and work there until about 2 o'clock, only arriving home with barely time to shave, shower and change into my police uniform and be ready to commence duty at 3pm.

Nightshift was probably the most punishing of all. After guarding, patrolling and watching all night long, I would snatch a quick breakfast before the family were even up, pack a lunch box and head off for the holding. After mixing and laying concrete for the next eight hours or so, I returned home shattered, had a meal and a shower before enjoying at most, four hours sleep before starting the whole process all over again. It goes without saying, that on my 'days off' police duties, I spent most of the time at the holding, only enjoying brief and infrequent outings with my wife and family… even those became joys of the past after I acquired the livestock.

However I did enjoy one memorable day out with Annette on the 22nd June of that year, when we went to the **Royal Highland Agricultural Show** at Ingliston, situated on the western outskirts of Edinburgh. I had been to the show several times before but this was a red letter occasion as I was now a farmer (of sorts) and may even purchase a thing or two. My cheque book, or rather my overdraft, was extremely modest compared to my fellow farmers, but what the heck, I was now one of that exclusive band.

I was unlikely to attract the salesmen on the stands which bore mighty tractors, milking parlours, cubic houses or Landrover vehicles and the like, but I could browse amongst the smaller more modest items and not feel out of place.

On one stall stood a very smart little high-sided livestock trailer, in battleship grey, with a proper ramp tailgate. Now that was something substantial which I needed and could afford on my overdraft. I raised and lowered the tailgate, lifted the drawbar to test its manoeuvrability and generally displayed genuine interest. Consequently, I was approached from both sides by eager salesmen...

"If sir is interested, I could allow a slight discount on that actual trailer if you could agree to leave it on display until the end of the show," said the older man. To be the owner of a trailer that was actually exhibited at this prestigious event... now that would indeed be something for a small time pig keeper (to be) and with a pathetic attempt at beating him down on price, I agreed to part with the princely sum of £99. But was I proud to produce my chequebook drawn on **West Latch Pig Farm** account, flourishing the signed page as I handed it over. I bet that salesman was impressed!

I then swaggered about in the knowledge of at long last belonging to the farming fraternity. Being one of the last big spenders, I parted with a further £42.24p for drinking cubes and creep feeders. Having said that, I shudder to think what some of the 'big boys' spent that day but that was of no concern of mine.

What does concern me now is the absolute knowledge that in every case they extracted a better deal than I did on each of their purchases! I never was and never will be a business man, as true business men always buy cheap and sell dear. I have always managed to get that philosophy the wrong way round.

However, I had done what I had set out to do on that fine June day and a few days later, at the close of the show, I returned to uplift my shiny new trailer and took it back to my little acre of heaven.

I see from the sole item of reference which I still possess, an immaculately written account book in Annette's beautiful handwriting, that I purchased a further 25kgs of Snowcem from **Portland Cement** for the modest price of £6.79p... I really went to town on the whitening of the piggery walls. I wanted my piggery to match, if not better, any other in the country for cleanliness. It was also rather therapeutic because there was so much improvement to be seen for so little cost and relatively little effort. A bucket of Snowcem and a very large brush, enabled me to effect a visual transformation in a short time. My attitude to whiteness and thus cleanliness stemmed from my days as a dairyman when the byre walls were regularly whitewashed and the steadings and gangways scrubbed down numerous time each day. I intended to maintain the same standards in my fledgling piggery.

With the imminent arrival of my pigs, on 30th July, I hitched up my brand new trailer and drove into Edinburgh, or to be more precise, Leith where the premises of **McGregor & Co.** were situated, to purchase 10cwt of sow meal. A row of enormous lorries were lined up outside the mill, each ready to gobble up at least 10 tons of meal and I feared that I would have to wait until they had been attended to, but to my surprise and delight, I had not long placed my order in at the office when a storeman indicated that he wished me to reverse my trailer in a side door where the ten bags awaited me. Was glad of my earlier experience on the farm where I had practised reversing two wheeled trailers. Consequently, I managed to place it neatly at the first attempt and no sooner had I disembarked when the first of my bags appeared down a chute. With the help of the storeman, we had them safely on the trailer in no time at all and I was on my way. I cannot speak too highly of the pleasure it was to deal with that Firm. There was I, buying small quantities initially but was treated just as promptly and courteously as any of their other customers.

If I had made it big in pigs and McGregors had still been extant, I would have continued to buy from them come what may. I have a natural loyalty towards anyone or business which does right by me which is probably why I am a failed businessman to this day. Apparently loyalty does not pay the bills… how sad.

CHAPTER FIVE

(The Pigs Arrive)

In 1973 there was a very successful pig multiplication unit at **Kamehill, East Fortune** run by a **William Cunningham,** producing breeding stock and it was from that source that I secured my first pigs.

I note that on 1st August, I bought ten Large White gilts and a Landrace boar, which set my overdraft back a further £460.00. My little livestock trailer was too small for such a load, so the vendor agreed to deliver the pigs the following day. I returned home with 5cwt of pig meal on my trailer and a huge grin on my face.

The following morning I was up at the holding at the crack of dawn. When I bought the place, I fell heir to quite a quantity of baled hay and in no time at all, I had the pens scrubbed out and deeply bedded with fresh straw in readiness for the new arrivals. I can still feel the surge of excitement as the lorry backed into the yard towards the access race I had constructed with wooden gates. In two shakes of a lamb's or in this case a pig's tail, I had my new charges safely settled into their new home.

I put the young boar in a pen between those containing the gilts in order that in due course his presence would help to bring them into season and indicate when that had occurred. It worked a treat, but in the meantime he had the social experience of being able to see them and more importantly, smell them. Within a matter of minutes it was as if they had been there for months... the last piece of the jigsaw had finally been put into place.

My modest holding now resounded to the gentle grunting of contented pigs, but I must admit to a degree of trepidation in the realisation that I was now solely responsible for the wellbeing of all those animals. Not unlike the feelings parents experience when they take home a new infant from the maternity hospital for the first time and realise that it is totally dependent on them for its survival!

At that time, my wife and I were the proud parents of three fine sons, therefor I feel justified making the comparison.

I walked up and down the piggery revelling in the fact that I was now a farmer on a commercial basis. Having said that, I was well aware that I had to link the aesthetic pleasure to profit in light of my steadily mounting overdraft.

If it was to be profit rather than loss, I had to get these young gilts 'in pig' as soon as possible, accepting that nature would also have to take its course. I could not set a date as I was now a mere observer watching for signs which would indicate that it would be fruitful for a certain gilt to be introduced to the boar. They were all old enough and large enough, therefor I had to be aware when each came on heat.

I remember well the morning when I entered the piggery and found a gilt standing against the dividing wall between her pen and the boar's, with her ears upright and touching above her head, with all the other gilts showing great interest in her... a clear indication of oestrus. I persuaded her to leave her pen for another I had prepared earlier, having covered the floor with sand to help minimise slipping. She had all the signs of readiness, was reluctant to move, her vulva was swollen, the characteristic elevation of the ears and even her little curly tail was askew to ease access.

The boar needed no encouragement to follow me along the gangway to the 'boudoir'. It was not the ideal to have both the gilt and boar as first timers anymore than it is with humans, but needs must. The boar's first attempt is always unpredictable, the difference between the male and female roles is obvious... she only requires to be passive and obliging whereas his performance requires a degree of skill and obvious enthusiasm. However, I need not have worried about the latter, it was there in abundance. She had his undivided attention and he sniffed eagerly at the appropriate places but his lack of experience did show somewhat when he tried to mount her head! Trying not to embarrass him too much, I guided him around until he had at least the possibility of a productive entry. He seemed to sense that he was on the verge of something most enjoyable and his penis began to protrude from its sheath.

Now, not for mere tittilation but rather for the benefit of those unfamiliar with a pig's anatomy, his penis is not like the usual blunt instrument, but more akin to a corkscrew with a delicate flexible tip which can quite easily penetrate an orifice in which it would be completely non productive... and a complete waste of semen. Therefor it indicates no perversion on the part of the pig-man, especially with an inexperienced boar, to help guide the tip into the appropriate venue for conception to occur.

That is exactly what I did and when he realised that mission was accomplished, he entered into the discharge phase with unbridled relish. What a boar lacks in girth, it makes up for in length and is corkscrewed for the entire distance.

My young boar did not hold back in any way and the gilt showed every sign of pleasure throughout the entire process. She stood stock still bearing his considerable weight without complaint, while grunting contentedly as his not inconsiderable load was discharged. Some animal matings are extremely brief or brutal affairs, but the pig's performance is more akin to humans. When the job was completed, he just lay quietly on her back enjoying the moment and when he eventually slid back onto all fours, his corkscrew twitched in the dying embers of gratification before disappearing back into its sheath.

He required little encouragement to leave his concubine and return to his pen, but I swear he had a swagger in his stride which I had never seen before. The gilt meanwhile, was a little more reluctant to move. I do not know if it was shell shock or the remnants of her hormone programming, but I had to leave her for a minute or two to compose herself before she was prepared to rejoin her friends.

Recounting this episode reminds me of the joke the old farmer used to tell when I was a farm lad. He said that a very posh family visited his farm and a young man had requested to help about the place. He was a bit dubious but relented and asked the young man to take a sow to the boar to be served. The young man duly obliged and a while later when asked if the mating had been a success, he replied, "top ho, sir... top ho," to which the old farmer was heard to mumble, "I just knew he would make an arse of it."

I digress again. Returning to the mating it was always my habit to allow a second service about twelve hours later, provided the sow was still amenable. There was no proof that the practice resulted in an increase in the size of the subsequent litter, but I always felt that it should and the boar certainly never objected to the increase in his workload.

I was backshift on the day in question therefor on completion of my shift at 11pm, I drove over to the holding where I removed the gilt from her pen and as I walked her along the passageway, I touched her back and she immediately stopped and elevated her ears.

"Well, no doubt about her still being on heat," I muttered as she took up her stance in the consummation pen. The boar practically galloped along the passageway and there was no doubt in his mind as to the purpose of his disturbed sleep. He set about the foreplay with relish, practically lifting the entranced gilt completely off her feet with his snout as he pummelled her belly. Having exhausted his interest in that area, he concentrated on the business end and launched himself onto her back in style. I merely observed this time as he docked successfully and looked with envy at his awesome thrusting motion. If anything, he dallied even longer on her back after the deed was done and as she seemed agreeable, I allowed him to dismount in his own good time.

Throughout the next couple of months, the gilts all came into heat in turn and the young boar had a whale of a time. Far from diminishing as his workload increased, his enthusiasm matched his endless energy and straightforward technique. Gone was the endless sniffing and prodding, it was straight down to business. On one occasion, through my fault, I took him to a gilt which was not quite fully on heat. She stood at his approach but moved forward each time he attempted to mount her, denying him penetration. Before I could abort the mating, he pinned her in a corner and unable to mount from the rear, climbed onto her shoulder and ejaculated into thin air. That was when I discovered just how much semen a boar produced and it is no wonder sows have such large litters. A few hours later she stood beautifully and the boar, fully replenished, completed his duty once more.

Throughout that autumn, I was a happy stockman. The sheer pleasure I derived from seeing my pigs flourish is indescribable. While I was busy around the steading, I often let the gilts out into the paddock and they sure enjoyed themselves rooting about in the earth and basking in the pre-winter sunshine. I am not sure if it was a blessing or not but having driven ten miles from home to the piggery, I always felt obliged to do more work than merely attending to the pigs. I carried on with the various renovation projects which were not immediately pressing and had the farrowing house and rearing pens completed in plenty of time.

I have previously mentioned that the water supply was drawn from a private spring and was not always reliable. So, to solve the problem, I bought a 500 gallon tank from a neighbouring farmer, who included delivery in the price, for which I was extremely grateful. Having said that, I was left with the problem of installing it on my own. It is amazing how, when working unaided, we learn to cope with tasks singlehandedly which ideally call for two people. I managed to roll the tank into the utility shed using round logs and then by means of patience, two car jacks and a pile of slab wood, I raised it three feet off the ground into the required position and built brick pillars at either end. When the cement had set, I carefully lowered the tank onto the brick piers, fitted a tap and ballcock and hey presto, I had myself water pressure when required for feeding and washing down the piggery.

Something was still missing in my new found country life, an appropriate dog and what could be more in keeping than a Border Collie. On my rounds in the police, I became aware of a beautiful litter of pups at **Blegbie Farm, Humbie**, farmed by the Lowrie family so off I set to view the pups. There were still several for which homes were sought and I came away with a pretty little bitch which I named **Bess**. I enjoyed her company for sixteen years. She grew up with my children and was my constant companion at the piggery. Long after I had admitted defeat in my agricultural venture, she still accompanied me on long countryside walks which filled in some of the time previously taken up by the pigs and still left me with family time.

During those walks I began to compose poems and formulate subjects for prose, a habit I still do to this very day. When Bess died, I thought that was a painful experience, but only six months later my lovely wife Annette died of cancer at the age of fifty and that was when I realised what real pain was.

CHAPTER SIX

(The Births)

Of course in 1973, I had no inkling of the sorrow which lay ahead and was excited at the prospect of my gilts farrowing. To make life as comfortable and natural for them, they had the run of the grassy paddock with access to a deeply strawed basement area under the grain store in which to rest and sleep. Because they had been together since birth, there was never any squabbling or aggressive behaviour within the group and they all lay snuggly together in the shelter overnight.

A sow's gestation period is three months, three weeks and three days... just under four months and as the weeks passed, I watched them swell in the appropriate places. I may also add, although by rights I should have mentioned it first, that I was also watching my lovely wife Annette swell in similar fashion, as she too was pregnant, but not for the first time. She was expecting our fourth child and as she had a five month start, it became clear that she and my first gilt would give birth about the same time, namely just before Christmas.

The logistical difficulties such a coincidence would throw up were not lost on us but with the over confidence of youth, we or more precisely I was sure that we could take it all in our stride. Annette was not quite so sure. She, being experienced at the mothering business, had all the preparations in place on the home front and I had the maternity suite ready up at the holding.

With about a week to go, I put the first gilt due into the farrowing house. By that stage in her pregnancy she was quite happy to spend most of the day at rest and found the cosiness of the crate not bad at all. The false ceiling, insulated floor and draught proofing made for a warm environment and in December, in the foothills of the Lammermuirs that was not a bad place to be.

I allowed her out for exercise while I mucked out and she seemed only too pleased to return to the warmth of the crate when available. I started the leave the creep heat lamp on when I left, just in case she came early. To say that my life was hectic is the understatement of the year. I was carrying our my policing duties, visiting the piggery twice a day while trying to take some of the domestic pressure of my long suffering wife, not to mention the obvious anxiety I had over her imminent labour.

About 7.30am on 17th December my wife announced that it was about time she headed for the maternity hospital in Edinburgh. I telephoned her sister Margot, who had agreed to look after our boys in a crisis and dropped them off at her house *en route* for the good old **Elsie Inglis**. Having arrived in time, I waited anxiously in the waiting room while her condition was assessed by the staff. It was decided that she would not give birth for some time as her contractions had weakened and she had stepped back from the brink as it were.

We held hands and kissed repeatedly for several minutes then she insisted that I leave and attend to the thousand and one things awaiting me at home. In those sensible days, husbands were not encouraged to be present at the birth and only the pushy ones insisted on that ridiculous privilege. I certainly had no wish to witness my wife's severe discomfort and to this day, hold on to that view. What in my humble opinion, the wife requires at that time is professional help and support, not a twittering, fawning imbecile who is only getting in the way. In any case, the wife is far too busy with the job in hand for his presence to have any relevance. There was also the small matter of my dayshift police duties and I was already three hours late!

Having left the medical staff the telephone number of the police station, I returned to Haddington and busied myself with paperwork in the office and to be close to a telephone... no mobiles in those days. I telephoned the hospital on the hour, every hour and just before I was due to finish my shift, I learned that Annette had given birth to a daughter and that both were well.

With a renewed spring in my step, I dashed to the shops to buy the ubiquitous card, flowers and chocolates before rushing home to tell my sons the good news. Without pausing for a meal, I rushed to the piggery to feed the pigs and to check on the mother-to-be. Her appearance and actions indicated an imminent start to the proceedings, but I was unable to remain with her, much as I desperately wished to do so. A precious wife and lovely daughter awaited me in Edinburgh therefor, after making the gilt as comfortable as possible, it was home for a quick shower, change of clothing, a hastily gulped down snack and into the car again for the long drive into Edinburgh.

It was our fourth child but the feeling of immense joy, pride and gratitude that my lovely wife and child were well, did not diminish as the size of our brood increased. Annette looked radiant, an absolute miracle after the day she had endured, but there was no sign of our daughter…

"She's lovely Harry," Annette said, adding, "the nurses take the babies to the nursery overnight so that the mothers can get a well earned rest and only bring them to the bedside for feeding." That seemed an eminently sensible procedure to adopt, I thought and immersed myself in loving exchanges with Annette. We settled on names for the new arrival, Constance Caroline and I enquired caringly about the trauma of the day, handed over the gifts and told her about all the good wishes I had received as the news got around. It never occurred to me to ask to see my daughter, assuming the staff were far too busy to bother with a doting father disturbing the silence in the nursery.

I was well aware that I would see the baby the following morning and no doubt she would still look the same. I stayed until I sensed that my continued presence was hindering the staff on their late evening duties and after kissing my wife tenderly, I left the hospital.

To this very day my daughter still teases me that she has been scared for life due to my failure to admire her on the day of her birth, but in all honesty, I thought that I would be a nuisance to the staff by asking them to bring her for inspection when they were such busy people. I have assiduously tried to avoid being a nuisance to people all my life… it is just the way I am, but Annette and Connie failed to see it that way, *c'est la vie.*

It was after nine o'clock in the evening as I headed for the piggery. My mind was a galaxy of thoughts — the health of my wife and new born, my three wonderful wee sons at home, the anticipation of a lovely Christmas with all my family around me and the additions due to my little pig herd.

The Christmas theme kept coming to the fore as I left the town lights and reached the peace of the little country roads leading to my holding. Free from the light pollution I could admire the stars twinkling in the dark blue night sky and with the temperature plummeting, the prospect of a really frosty night was assured.

How well everything was dovetailing into a quite remarkable day and I could see the frost already glinting on the roadway in front of me. I must admit to singing, 'White Christmas' albeit not very well, as I drew into the piggery yard. My feet crunched on the frozen ground and my breath hung in clouds as I approached the farrowing house and slid the door open.

Closing the door quickly behind me to conserve heat and even before I could lift the draught screening to enter into the inner area, I could hear the high pitched squeaks coming from the new born piglets. The place was so warm and the heating lamps gave off such a cosy glow. I counted six beautiful pink silken piglets attached to their mother's teats with her lying comfortably on her side. She was uttering the most reassuring little grunts to her new family, each grunt sending a ripple along her belly which almost dislodged the youngsters from the milk bar.

I was extremely relieved to see that there were no still-borns lying at her rear and no sign of the afterbirth.

"Not quite finished yet, are you lass?" I whispered.

Drawing up a bale of straw I sat in the shadows and watched enthralled at the delightful cameo being played out in the warm lamplight. I hardly had time to absorb the miracle of creation when the gilt's grunting changed to something less soothing than hitherto and she began to pedal with her hind legs, drawing them up towards her body. The piglets were in grave danger of receiving an accidental kick, so I removed them from her teats and placed them directly under the lamp in the creep area. Having benefitted from a little nourishment they formed a neat little circle in the warmth and closed their tiny blue eyes.

The thought of multiple births make a women's eyes water, I know that thought had passed through Annette's mind earlier in the day, but there is quite an upside to it. An animal giving birth to a litter of offspring experiences a number of lesser pains rather

Page 62

than the one severe trauma and as if to underline that assertion, within a minute or two and without any apparent discomfort another little piglet popped out. She certainly did not bellow aloud as cows do when calving, or women for that matter. The piglet's siblings had fared all right unattended, but as I happened to be on hand, I lifted it up, pulled the sac from its head, cleared the mucus from its mouth and gave it a little slap on the back. It coughed and spluttered for a moment and then appeared to breathe normally.

I was so thrilled at last to be a pig farmer with my stock beginning to multiply. A further two piglets were born before the afterbirth came away... job now done. Nine beautiful little piglets and a mother performing her maternal duties as per nature intended, what more could anyone ask for?

Her grunting had now returned to the comforting little sounds she had been making when I arrived. That was obviously a signal the piglets inherently understood as they left the comfort of the heat lamp and booked a teat each, the stronger ones claiming the foremost milk outlets and the weaker or smaller siblings being left with those towards the rear end of the mother. Once they had staked their claims, that teat was now theirs for as long as they suckled, which is why the gap between the largest and smallest tended to increase because there is always more milk in the forward teats... just another wonderful example of nature making sure of the survival of the species.

If food for the sow was in short supply, the bigger piglets would always survive while the smaller ones would perish... much the same as birds feeding the largest chicks first. Nature can appear to be cruel but it is normally effective. Having acknowledged that fact, it would have been nice from the stockman's point of view, if the smaller piglets had received the extra feeding and perhaps evened up the litter, but that is man wishing again to interfere with nature.

I was impressed to see the way that the inexperienced gilt even rolled slightly onto her back in order to expose both rows of teats to her babies. How about that for maternal instinct and yet we often hear so much today about all the information required by expectant mums... what baloney!

It was the end of a perfect day. I sat until well after midnight just admiring the contented little family scene. Eventually, I dragged myself away after ensuring that the gilt had plenty fresh water at her head.

The cold night air caught my breath after the steamy warmth of the farrowing house. Having swapped the rosy glow for the cold steely blue of a frosty landscape, I stood awhile admiring the crystal dust scattered over the trees and shrubs, the heavenly spectacle clearly visible in the clean, unpolluted air at the foot of the Lammermuir Hills.

It felt great to be alive!

CHAPTER SEVEN

(Business Boomed)

It was a wonderful Christmas and New Year period, but for the first time there was no possibility of a full day off with the family. Each and every day for the next four years I had to drive the round trip of some twenty miles to tend to my livestock. I often thought how much better it would have been to have had them on my doorstep when a few minutes work would have sufficed, then back into the bosom of my family, but that was not to be.

Within a week or two of the first farrowing, my little holding was alive with the sounds of young piglets as each gilt produced a healthy litter. Working alone had one great drawback… there are some jobs which are extremely tricky for one person to do singlehandedly but never was there a truer saying than 'necessity being the mother of invention'. I have already given the example of the difficulty I had in raising the water tank on my own, but with the arrival of the little pigs I was faced with the dilemma of how to administer injections and carry out castrations alone. I have always considered myself to be one of life's *'autolycus'*, the character in Shakespeare's play **'The Winter's Tale'** who was a 'snapper up of unconsidered trifles', that is to say that I never overlooked anything which was going free. It just may come in handy someday, even if it's value is doubtful at the time.

A few months earlier on one of my nightshift prowls, I had spotted a little hospital trolley which had been deposited in a skip outside the local hospital which was undergoing renovation. With my *autolycus* hat on, I just knew that it would come in handy someday so I liberated it from the skip and relocated it in a shed at the piggery.

It consisted of a wheeled frame with a lower shelf and a combined upper shelf and wash basin. I remembered it when I began to make plans for the wellbeing of the litters and was faced with the tasks as aforesaid. To solve this, I removed the upper shelf from the trolley and replaced it with two lengths of doweling about two inches apart which gave me a very successful little operating table for the piglets. When a piglet had its hind legs slipped between the doweling rods it was suspended head down, unable to struggle, quite comfortable and in the perfect position to carry out procedures with both hands free. It made what could have been a very difficult duty much more pleasant for me and less traumatic for the piglets. The instruments were to hand in a disinfectant solution in the bin which made for a very professional operation. All in all, I was very proud of that little invention of mine.

Spurred on by my successful breeding programme, I decided to increase my breeding stock when on a visit to **Spilmersford Mains Farm.** I learned from John Hood that he had two surplus gilts and was about to market them as bacon pigs. I quickly snapped them up at £36 each (bacon prices) and took them back to **West Latch**.

About the same time, I went to the fat stock market in Edinburgh because I had heard that cast sows went under the hammer at **Swans Market**. Cast sows being those which are deemed past their productive years, are not producing the goods insufficient numbers or, as I later sadly swelled their numbers, are being disposed of because their owners are forced out of business. Those unfortunate animals are destined for the processing sector of the business and invariably end up as sausages or hamburgers.

I saw this huge **Landrace** sow which looked suspiciously like she was in pig and on impulse, bought her at a very reasonable price. It was certainly her lucky day. Instead of ending up in the slaughterhouse, I took her home to a nice cosy pen at the holding. She repaid me handsomely with a fine litter of ten piglets about a month later and went on to have a further three or four litters before meeting the 'grim reaper'.

Thirteen sows all becoming pregnant to a fine boar and my rearing pens full of young pigs, I was in seventh heaven. As of 31st March, my overdraft stood at £2,626.72p but my business plan was still on course. Although I was nearing my limit, my pens were full of pigs which were fast approaching store weight and would soon be bringing in sizeable cheques. Not a minute too soon, because servicing my overdraft was costing £30 each month plus regular payments of £250 to **McGregors** for complete pig food and starter pellets. Because of the relatively secure position I was in, I was upbeat and coping with the ever increasing workload not too badly. My family rarely saw more than fleeting glances of me, but as ever my darling Annette was a tower of strength and a very capable (single) parent to our children. She never complained and seemed to have convinced the children that it was quite normal for their father to be absent from the home so much. They were always cheerie enough when I did have a moment or two with them.

The 29th March was a red-letter day for me and was probably the summer of my success in pig breeding. The remainder of my stockman's career would best be described as stoicism in the face of adversity. However, let me bask for a moment in the sunshine of that day. I had arranged for **G. T. Roberts** to send a lorry to uplift twenty store pigs, that number being far too many for my trailer to cope with.

I was up at the piggery at dawn, had bedded those pigs destined for market in deep clean straw the day previously and mucked them out immediately on arrival before they could dirty themselves. My efforts were rewarded, not only were they spotless although I say it myself, they were an even bunch in both size and conformation — a really fine pen of pigs.

Although ultimately destined for the slaughterhouse, I was sending them on to a market where they would be sold to another pig-man with the resources to take them on to the heavier bacon weight. I was confident that they would fetch a good price as I fed them their breakfast.

The hurdles were in place to make a loading race and the passageways clean when I heard the lorry entering the yard. Preparation is the key word when intending to move pigs and I had left them no option other than to run up into the back of the lorry. No trauma, no marked pigs, no swearing and a very happy lorry driver.

I more or less followed the lorry away from **West Latch**, but I headed for home to change into what I thought a farmer should wear at market — tweed jacket, flannel shirt, cord trousers and polished shoes.

"I've never seen you so excited," said Annette, as I gulped down a cup of tea and a home baked scone.

"I've never been heading for market to see my stock being sold before," I replied and kissed her goodbye.

I felt ten feet tall as I strode into **Swans Market** that morning. I located my pigs and they looked well in their holding pen. I was so proud to acknowledge being their owner to other pig men when asked as they toured the pens. Some were dealers, some were other pig men looking to buy and others were like myself, sellers just eyeing up the opposition. I really felt like shouting it from the rafters but we farmers do not behave like that... we play our cards very close to our chest.

I was very heartened by some of the comments I overheard around the pen and the fact that I had drawn a lot in the middle of the sale was also encouraging. Eventually it was my turn and my pigs were herded into the sale ring by the drovers...

"Come on now gentlemen, here is a fine pen of pigs from **West Latch**... a new enterprise producing fine stock... who will start me off at £10?" implored the auctioneer. I stood there as proud as punch listening to my very own pigs going under the hammer. "£9 then, thank you, I'm bid £9, £9.20p, £9.40p, £9.60p, £9.80p, against you at the back... £10, thank you, £10.20p, £10.40p,£10,60p, my bid is at the front... £10.80p, £11, £11.20p, £1140p, £11.60p,

£11.80p,£12… all finished at £12… sold to Mr Fraser."

Twelve pounds each… that was the best trade amongst the store pigs that morning… I was on cloud nine and I swear I swaggered as I walked into the market restaurant for a pie and pint with the other pigmen.

"Good trade you got today, lad… a fine pen of pigs," said an old hand at the game.

"Thanks, there are plenty more just like them at home," I said, rather too smugly for my own good.

"Make the most of it just now lad, because those bloody Danes are about to flood the Country with subsidised bacon," he added, bringing me down to earth with a bump and taking the gloss off the moment.

Little did I know how prophetic his words would prove. However, I had a very important duty to perform… I walked into

Swans Office shoulder to shoulder with the other big boys and when it was my turn to approach the cashier, I received a cheque for £301.89p. At long last there was something to enter on the credit side of my balance sheet and just in time to go some way in placating that bank manager.

But my real wage earning duties awaited me and lucrative pig farmer or not, a late shift in uniform awaited me at Haddington. It was 11pm before I could put my feet up but at long last I had reached the stage when money was starting to come in as well as going out, but that cautionary remark by the old farmer still niggled away as I fell into bed for a much needed sleep.

CHAPTER EIGHT

(Storm Clouds Looming)

The spring of 1971 was hectic but pleasurable. When I come to think of about it, at no time during those four years was it anything but hectic. I had some sows successfully in pig again and I had my pens full of young pigs, all at various stages.

Although the incoming bills were worrying, I did have collateral security on the hoof as it were. I note that I put one hundred store pigs through the market from the first litters, which averaged out at about eight pigs per litter. That from gilts and a novice stockman was not bad going.

Springtime has a habit of putting a spring in your step at the best of times, but I must say that I really enjoyed my time at the piggery in the early months of that year. I could not get over the thrill of having my own pigs and seeing them thriving so well.

Granted, small numbers do allow more time for individual attention but when considering all the other calls on my time, it was no mean feat devoting what precious time I did have to the extra comfort and attention I lavished on my stock.

It is a very true saying that, 'a change is as good as a rest' and I put that to the test on a daily basis.

I would keep switching from one job to another throughout the day, if I had the luxury of a full day at **West Latch**. After feeding and mucking out, I would alternate between mixing meal by hand, weighing batches of pigs, castrating youngsters, building conversion or maintenance, clearing blocked drains and general stockmanship. That last item was the important time spent just walking around the pens watching the pigs' behaviour to spot any early signs of trouble.

I would spend the stockmanship time adding to the comfort and wellbeing of the pigs, allowing batches of weaners out into the grass paddock in turn to gambol in the fresh air and for those which could not be released, I would pull up great divots, give them to the ones inside and watch as they tore them apart looking for tasty morsels. Apart from the pleasure it gave me, it prevented boredom in the pigs and I never had an incident of tail or ear biting, which is the plague of some intensively managed piggeries and can lead to substantial losses.

Pigs are lovely beasts, intelligent, playful, human friendly and trusting. They will rub against you when entering their pen, tug at your jacket sleeve and stand in seventh heaven as you scratch their backs or rub their ears. However, they can also be extremely aggressive to each other and for no apparent reason they can turn on one of their own and if there is no one to intervene, they will worry it to death.

I am convinced that boredom was the root of that vice, although, hand on heart, I never had that problem, thank God and I am convinced it was because I took the time to make life as happy for them as possible.

It is plain to see that I love pigs and would dearly have wished that I could have continued to breed them, but even as I spent the beautiful spring of that year surrounded by healthy pigs, storm clouds were beginning to loom on the horizon. My finances were not too healthy with my overdraft expenditure standing close to my limit and that was after selling most of my first batch of store pigs. I was entering another lean period for sales and an extended period of expenses.

The price I was receiving for my pigs was dropping due entirely to the predacious nature of the Danish marketing strategy, as predicted by the old farmer. Anyone over a certain age will remember the concerted advertising campaign they mounted to pursued the UK housewife to buy Danish bacon. Their pig farmers were heavily subsidised and thus able to ship consignments of bacon over here and still undercut our prices. That was something I had been unable to foresee and allow for in my initial business plan when I set out on my pig venture.

To compound my difficulties, there was an increase in cereal prices, the major component of pig food. I had no land on which to grow barley to cushion the effects of reduced returns. Consequently, I had to buy in 100% of the food I fed to my pigs at well nigh extortionate prices, while watching housewives queuing up daily at the shops to buy Danish bacon. Every newspaper I picked up contained the advertisement for imported bacon and my television, when I had time to view, repeatedly displayed that infuriating logo accompanied by those sickening jingles extolling the affordability of Danish bacon.

I reassured myself that pig returns were notorious for having peaks and troughs and if I could just hang on, things would get better…

I was actually optimistic that things would improve. I still enjoyed the experience of having my own little piece of heaven. **West Latch** was my little kingdom, tucked away in the foothills of the Lammermuir Hills in a sparsely populated area. It was where I could retreat to and be immersed in my rural idyll. It was extremely beautiful there, with the rolling hills as a backdrop with marginal pasture around the steading.

Whenever I got out of the car, I was met by the most invigorating fresh air. On hearing my arrival, there broke out what I can only describe as raucous impatience. The squealing was ear shattering and I can well understand why people would be reluctant to live next to a piggery because of the noise. Having said that, it only lasted a matter of minutes until I could get the meal into their troughs, whereupon the sound changed to a marvellous slurping chorus which could not be overheard outwith the building, but was a treat to listen to. Pigs really eat their food with relish.

I can hear some of you saying that whilst the noise may have subsided, it is the smell which is objectionable as it is there all the time. I would have to take issue with that. Contrary to ignorant belief, the pig is a very clean animal in its habits and keeps its sleeping quarters free from filth. Even in a square unpartitioned pen, if clean straw is placed in one half, the pigs will all dung in the unneeded section and keep their bedding unsoiled. Not only does that save on bedding material, but it makes mucking out a much quicker and easier chore.

As I mentioned earlier, I was fortunate in that **West Latch** was packed with straw when I took over and I never scrimped on bedding. In regard to the muck heaped outside and then spread on the fields, which you might conclude gives rise to the stench, I have to say that animal excrement mixed with straw and allowed to mature is a most wonderful plant food and I am afraid that if it offends, then the countryside is not the best place to live. But slurry… now that is a different matter altogether!

I enjoyed mucking out as it brought out the playful streak in the pigs. They would often grip the shovel shaft in their mouth, nibble at the cuff of my sleeve or hem of my jacket and should I remonstrate with them in mock anger, they would bowff at me and scamper to the back of the pen. I loved the way they watched me with their beady little eyes. Some sows became real characters, they would rub up against my legs or nudge me with their snouts to encourage me to scratch their ears.

I was not unduly sentimental, but the fact that they would ultimately be sent for slaughter, in my mind made it all the more desirable that they were treated well and with humanity.

And pleasures do not come much better than the short periods I spent sitting in the sunshine in the yard eating my packed lunch. I could hear the insects humming as they busied themselves in the weeds along the wall base and watched the magnificent aerial display of the swallows in pursuit of their meal. Winter was an altogether different scenario, but again the fact that I was in the relative comfort of the buildings, when I could hear the wind howling or the sleet battering on the roof, brought feelings perhaps more akin to relief rather that pleasure, but an inner joy nonetheless. But summer or winter, I did not sit for long. By the time I was on to tea and biscuits, I was invariably on the move again with cup in hand, walking between the pens planning my next task.

Wintertime if anything, gave me more satisfaction because the more atrocious the weather was, the greater the relief it was to gain the bield afforded by the building and the realisation that all my stock was cosy and safely indoors. The new born piglets under the heating lamps could tell me if I had the conditions right. If they were piled up on top of one another, then they required more heat and I would lower the lamps. Conversely, if there was a space under the lamp and the piglets were scattered, it was too low and required to be raised. If on the other hand, they were just lying in an orderly fashion side by side, then I had it just right.

The farrowing house was particularly cosy due to my ad hoc insulation which was proving most effective. That is where I chose to have lunch in the winter, sat on a bale of straw watching a sow feeding her little ones. She would sing to them as they lined up along her belly and latched on to their chosen teats.

With hindsight, that experience alone made all the hard toil worthwhile.

CHAPTER NINE

(Troubled Times)

Even as things got tougher, I still found comfort and fulfilment by watching the birth of a new litter of pigs. The rest of the world could go to hell and was of no consequence when I made myself comfortable in the farrowing house when a birth was due.

The atmosphere was cosy and intimate. The low ceiling, the warm glowing heating lamps, all draughts excluded by straw bales and plastic sheeting, provided a timeless bubble in which to witness the miracle of birth. Everything had been prepared in the fashion of nest building by an expectant woman. The farrowing crate was warm and dry, the sow was in good condition and no distractions were present.

The first pedalling motion by the sow heralded the onset of birth. At that point I was completely happy and contented with life. Nothing else mattered, such as money worries, foul weather, excessive workload or guilt at being absent from my family. All these things disappeared for a couple of blessed hours, as one after the other beautiful little silken piglets with cheeky eyes and curly tails were born. They uttered such delightful little squeaks as I checked each in turn before placing them under the heat lamp. The sow seemed so unperturbed by the event and willingly suckled her extended family immediately after the work was done.

Her gentle grunts rippled along her stomach line dislodging all but the most tenacious of her piglets from their teats, but undaunted those which had been detached immediately reclaimed their place at the banquet and suckled heartily. Right to the end of my unequal struggle against commercialism, I found solace in being present at a farrowing.

However, outwith those cameos of delight, life was getting pretty stressful. Regular bills in the region of £250 arrived from **McGregors** for pig meal. It was costing me about £25 each month to service my overdraft and approximately the same for fuel and routine maintenance on my car which was a gas guzzling estate. Trying to balance that with store pigs only fetching £10 each was becoming well nigh impossible and my overdraft just kept nudging towards its limit.

Something drastic had to be done. Not only was my time at home of ever reducing duration, but I know that I was a very edgy individual to live with due to sheer exhaustion and the increasing pressure I was under.

With the return on store pigs not even covering the cost of their feeding, I had to do something and soon. It is normal for farmers to discuss costs, negotiate and purchase grain at the corn exchange but there was no place there for someone wishing to deal in hundred weights not tons.

One day however, I wandered into **Sinclair McGill's** premises in **Sidegate** and bumped into Wullie, the mill foreman. I am pleased to report that I had the same pleasant experience there as I had at **McGregors** when I mentioned the smaller quantities I dealt in.

"No problem, Harry," said Wullie, "we can sell you barley by the bag... as little or as much as you need."

He was a pleasure to deal with and would often interrupt whatever he was doing to load a couple of bags onto my wee trailer whenever I called.

I see that I was paying £50 per ton for barley, much more affordable than the complete meal I had been buying, even after taking into account the concentrate I still had to purchase from **McGregors** to make the balanced feed and the milling of the barley at home.

This brings me nicely on to another gem of a person. **Mr Wylie of Wylie & Sons**, who operated mobile mills. I do not think there is such a service nowadays, but in those days which, let us face it, was only 4-5 decades ago, many small farmers and smallholders still required the services of a mobile mill.

As the name implies, it was a grinding mill and mixer mounted on a lorry chassis. I would wait until I had a ton or more of barley before arranging for a visit. Mr Wylie would park up in the yard as close as he could get to the granary and I would barrow out the barley concentrate. After the milling and mixing process, the complete meal was blown through a pipe back into the granary in bulk. I always tried to have the bags close to the door in readiness to save him time but occasionally I would be running late and rushing around preparing for him when he arrived.

"Man Harry, stop rushing with those heavy sacks or you'll kill yourself. I'm in no great hurry."

His sympathetic approach probably stemmed from the fact that he knew that I had either just come off nightshift or was about to start a backshift after my stint at the piggery. His prediction about the folly of rushing around proved substantial one day when I slipped with a 2cwt bag of barley on my back, twisted as I fell and damaged my back. The initial pain was excruciating and made working very uncomfortable for a good while. In fact, I still suffer recurring bouts of back pain to this day.

I had to thole it on the beat as well as continuing to look after my pigs, as my senior officers knew about my little enterprise and the fact that I had to look after them every day. I could hardly take time off policing duties while still attending to my pigs, so I struggled to suffer the back pain and the many other little mishaps which occur when engaged in manual work.

I remember the time when I accidentally stood on a rusty nail which was protruding from a piece of discarded timber. The nail pierced my rubber boot and lodged in the sole of my left foot. Whilst I managed to prise it free and take myself to the local hospital, I realised that I would need at least an anti-tetanus injection. As I was known to the staff there, I well remember a lovely nurse smiling as she filled a massive syringe...

"I've always wanted to plunge one of these into a policeman's bare bottom," she laughed.

At least I made her day and I have to say, that injury to my foot still troubles me and I have to visit a chiropodist periodically to deal with a corn which forms on the site of the nail puncture.

Although buying barley and milling on site had reduced the cost of feeding my pigs, the pathetic price I was receiving for my stock fell well short of covering that feeding, never mind all the other costs incurred. I was rearing large healthy litters; each of my sows was more than playing her part, but the irony was that the more pigs I produced the more money I lost... how can that possibly be just?

It was quite frankly, most unjust, but it was happening because our shores were open to cheap imports, an unfair fact that has fatally harmed many good businesses.

I tried everything I could think of to try and at least break even, ever hoping for better times to come. Wullie at McGills, like many others I was fortunate enough to have had dealings with, was understanding and when I collected a bag or two of good barley at the going rate, he would often throw in what was more or less rubbish... scrapings off the floor, stuff with not much nutritional value but which helped to bulk up the rations.

At that time there was a glut of potatoes and those taken out of the human food chain, were dyed purple and sold off cheaply for animal food. I obtained a load of these and as their food value increases by cooking them, I spent many hours I could ill afford, boiling spuds in an old electric boiler and then mixing the resultant mash with the barley meal. The enthusiasm with which the pigs attacked that food helped to compensate me for the extra work involved, but when I took into account the amount of electricity used, I was indeed caught in a vicious cycle... but my pigs had full stomachs.

I remember I learned that there was a load of condemned barley in **Guy's** yard in Haddington. The sample contained too many foreign weeds and to make matters worse, the tarpaulin on the lorry conveying the load had ripped, resulting in it becoming damp. I got it all for next to nothing. It was tipped out in one of their sheds and I spent many hours hand bagging and conveying it load by load in my little trailer to the piggery.

Once there, it was spread out on the grain store floor and turned repeatedly by hand shovel until it had dried out. It was then milled and mixed which greatly reduced my feed bills for a few weeks, but the extra work it had created was almost the proverbial straw that broke the pigman's back!

CHAPTER TEN

(The Move)

In the spring of 1975, I was working the piggery when in came **George Hodge** of **Humbie Mill Farm**. I was aware that he had bought the ground around the piggery from Stuart King and soon made me aware of the reason for his visit.

For the umpteenth time in my life, I allowed myself to be talked into doing something which I had not planned to do and, more importantly, did not wish to do.

To paraphrase what took place, George informed me that he had a purpose built piggery adjacent to his farm at Humbie which he no longer used and suggested that we might simply swap piggeries. His approach was motivated by a desire to obtain the buildings at **West Latch** to service the land he had recently bought, but emphasised that **Hazyhill** (the piggery at Humbie) could accommodate more pigs than mine and that it would be more accessible in inclement weather.

I did not require larger premises but the easier access did interest me, having just survived a testing winter period, so I agreed almost there and then for a cashless exchange between us, although I would need to fund my own legal expenses. A more shrewd businessman than I would of course have insisted that he meet all the legal fees since he clearly initiated the deal, but as you will have realised, I never have been and never will be a successful businessman.

For the life of me, I cannot negotiate to my benefit, so having agreed to his terms, I instructed a firm of solicitors in Haddington to act on my behalf. I am not naming the Firm for reasons which will become self evident later, suffice to say that yet again I became unstuck in financial matters.

It was agreed that I would take possession of **Hazyhill** around midsummer, which seemed to me to be a good idea as the move would entail the transportation of new born piglets. Consequently, the date was set for mid June and I arranged for a lorry from **G.T.Roberts** to transport all the sows and store pigs, whilst I crated all the little ones and in several journeys moved them by trailer to their new Humbie home, some three miles away.

What can never be depended upon in Scotland is the weather. It snowed, not a lot but enough to make the roads slushy and the temperature to drop. I suppose with the benefit of hindsight and the luck that I was having, it was something that should have been anticipated.

Hazyhill was indeed a purpose built piggery, but where **West Latch** had a charm and aesthetic beauty, it was completely functional and plain ugly… functional yes, but only as a fattening unit. I therefor had to start all over again and install farrowing crates, rearing pens and draught proofing whilst caring for a full compliment of pigs, all at the same time. If I remember correctly, I even took over the last sow and litter which George had in the piggery… at an inflated commercial valuation of course!

It probably was an easier to manage unit, consisting of two in-line buildings with pens on either side of a central gangway and a lean-to grain shed at one end, but I never formed an attachment to that place. Whereas I have often wished that I could have retained **West Latch**, even without the pigs, as it was somewhere pleasant to retreat to when I eventually retired from the police service.

We had agreed on comparative areas of ground around the two piggeries, but unlike **West Latch** with its little copse of trees and stone walls, the ground I received at **Hazyhill** was a rather relinquished awkward shaped banking surrounded by post and wire fencing. The place just did not have the appeal of that which I has hastily relinquished, but at the time I had far more to worry about than its appearance.

Having taken over the in-situ sow, my livestock now consisted of sixteen sows and all their progeny to store weight pigs which, although a modest number compared with most commercial units, entailed a great deal of work in addition to my professional duties. It was work that had to be done seven days a week, fifty-two weeks in the year and which was losing me money into the bargain.

Further cuts would have to be made and I decided that it was transportation costs which would fall to the axe.

Drastic problems call for drastic solutions, so I sold my car privately for £570, a sum which went straight into the bank to buy me a little more time. One problem tackled, another one created. I still needed to travel some twenty miles each day to service my pigs, so in anticipation of selling my car, I acquired free of charge, a dilapidated moped, although I note from my records that it actually cost me £13.97p to get it serviced and made roadworthy.

Twenty miles up hill and down dale in all weathers on a moped… I must have been really desperate and it is little wonder that I was edgy. I struggled through for a month and I see from these selfsame records that on 13th September, I bought a new 125cc Honda motor cycle registered number WSS 87N from **Pow Motor Cycles, Tranent.** Mercifully, I had negotiated a helmet and weatherproof clothing with the deal. The purchase was on credit of course, but the moderate repayments and the economy of fuel consumption was a mighty relief compared to my previous travel costs. One more problem dealt with but yet another one created... I was left with no means of transporting anything other than myself.

But into the breach stepped the genial **Geordie Roberts.** I cannot praise that man high enough. He was a giant of a man physically, with a large rotund figure, round red face and with eyes which sparkled but with a mouth which often offended. A rough diamond of a man but a good friend, Geordie did not suffer fools gladly but admired effort and ambition. He could not get over the hours I was putting in and what I had managed to achieve single-handed. When he heard that the Council had turned down my application to build a house at the piggery, he was intent on going into the offices to tell them a thing or two. I did not think that move would help my case and persuaded him otherwise. He had a record of altercations with officialdom, but what he did do for me was to cut the cost of transporting my pigs to market to an absolute minimum. His bills would be long overdue and when I expressed a worry about them mounting up, he would just laugh and agree to hit me with them the following week.

Sure enough an account would arrive but it did not reflect all the transport costs which he had provided. When I pointed this out, all he said was,

"Okay, we'll call it quits if you give Margot, his daughter, a couple of runts to fatten up for the freezer."

Margot duly arrived at the piggery but instead of giving her the poorest, I chose two of the best from the litter and gave them to her. I am a great believer in kindness being acknowledged and rewarded in this life rather than relying on it in the next.

Geordie continued to give me support to the end of my pig breeding venture and it was with great sadness that I learned of his untimely death a few years later.

For a full year I travelled back and forth each day to the new holding on the motor cycle. It was quite pleasant in the summer months but in the winter is was sheer hell. I was often going there very early in the morning or late a night before the snow ploughs had cleared the roads and I can tell you that was a hair-raising experience.

Sometimes I could not get up the hill at Humbie Mill and had to abandon the motor bike and complete the journey over the fields on foot to reach the piggery. Not just that, but rather than making life easier for myself, not having the use of my little trailer was proving ever more stressful.

Financially it had taken the weight off my shoulders but I was paying the price physically. It was bad enough to jump into the car at all odd hours when dog tired and head for the holding, but a motor cycle ride in the sleet and snow took its toll. It was just not the answer.

Our local garage had recently taken over the franchise for Lada cars, those cheap Russian no-frills vehicles and I bought a second hand one with a tow bar fitted for next to nothing. The sale of my motor cycle to a colleague more than paid for the car's deposit and I was once again a little bit more in control of events.

CHAPTER ELEVEN

(Butchering)

I had added a few hens to my little livestock enterprise and besides keeping the family in eggs, I had the odd half dozen to sell, but that was never going to get my finances out of the red. I had to get a bigger return for my pigs.

I knew of a farmer who was butchering his own pigs and selling the meat in quantity to people to stock their freezers... could that be my salvation, I wondered? I contacted **Frank Anderson**, a retired butcher of the old school and confirmed from him that he did in fact butcher animals for a few farmers on their premises and would be happy to help me out in that respect. His terms were quite specific, namely conveyance from his home to the piggery — once to kill and once again to joint the carcass when cool, a few quid pocket money and a stiff dram on each occasion. That was more than acceptable to me. I asked what preparations I required to put in place and a date was set for the first session. Not only did this arrangement offer a way of increasing my income but it afforded me the opportunity to step back in time as it were, to learn to be more self sufficient, a skill which was dying out even in the seventies.

On the day appointed, I picked up Frank in the early evening and drove him to the piggery. I had earlier identified the unfortunate animal to be slaughtered and justified my actions to myself in the knowledge that its peers would be off to the slaughterhouse within a day or two anyway and may not experience such a stress free end.

The pig selected, with no inkling of what was about to happen, was removed from the others and placed in an empty pen well away from the others and I dropped some meal onto the floor. As I said, Frank was a butcher from the old school and whilst the pig was engrossed in licking the floor clean, he stunned it with a severe blow to the forehead with a heavy hammer. It dropped immediately. Frank then cut its throat and pedalled its legs in order to pump out the blood quickly. I had no need to save the blood as I did not intend to make black puddings and so allowed it to seep into deep straw for composting. That was the worst over... what had been loveable animal was now dead and we were dealing with butcher meat. I felt better.

I already had hot water in the boiler as we lifted the carcass into a large tin bath, where I poured the hot water over it and then we set about scraping it with sharpened paidle heads (the head of a draw hoe) to remove the bristles. Frank pulled off the toenails with a hook he produced from his bag of knives and after a few minutes hard work the carcass was smooth and clean. It was then lifted out onto the pre-scrubbed floor where Frank deftly cut around the bung (anus) and tied off the intestines to prevent contamination. He then slit the carcass and gralloched it (removed all the internal organs) and the pluck (heart, kidneys, lungs and liver) was carefully hung up on a hook.

With the tendons exposed in the hind legs, a wooden peg was inserted between them and the carcass was hoisted up on a pulley which I had made ready. Frank then expertly opened the breast bone with a cleaver and wedged open the rib cage with another piece of wood, whereupon we flushed out the innards with cold water and then left it to drip and cool for the next twenty-four hours.

It really kindled in me a desire for complete self sufficiency to see that wonderful butcher meat hanging there, meat which a short time earlier had been a living animal. A squeamishness about killing and subsequently devouring what had been a living animal was put to rest. I felt that I had now something in common with my ancestors. I get that same feeling today when my Labrador brings me back an injured pheasant which I kill, pluck, draw and prepare for the pot. I call it survivalism.

However, back to the pig. I put the pluck into a bag and took it home after dropping Frank off at his house. The heart and lungs were cooked for the dogs and I had the liver and kidneys in the pan the following day for my lunch.

That evening, I again took Frank to **Hazyhill** where, on a trestle table I had prepared, he cut the carcass into joints. Some were boned and rolled, the back and loin made into chops and pride of place were the magnificent hams. Within half-an-hour what had been a pig carcass was now a crate full of the most delicious pork joints anyone could ever have wished for. Nothing was wasted. The bath chaps and trotters were delicious and as I stated, I had already consumed the liver and kidneys. There were no sweetbreads as the pig had been previously castrated.

People often turn up their nose at the cheaper cuts of meat, but that is because we are all too well off today. When I was a youngster living in Edinburgh, there were offal butcher shops which only dealt in the cheaper cuts and they were always busy. People do not realise that they actually eat offal when they consume sausages, hamburgers and the like, which are processed from the less desirable cuts of meat and as I said earlier, old sows.

Having jointed the meat for me, Frank got his well deserved dram and pocket money and I returned home with a crate of the finest pork. Annette was suitably impressed and delighted that our meat needs for the foreseeable future had been secured for relatively little cost. She told friends and neighbours and showed to them the various cuts of meat. Without exception, they all expressed surprise that it looked as though it was straight out of a butcher's shop... I don't know what they expected it to look like. That is the problem with certain quarters of the modern world, they cannot link meat to the living animal. There is a curtain behind the supermarket shelf which hides the source of meat from the housewife and her children. The knowledge, ability and willingness to process meat from the hoof to the pan is now largely missing. If it is not wrapped in shiny plastic and in a refrigerated counter, it is not recognised as edible. Unfortunately, children no longer see the whole carcasses of animals hanging up in butcher's shops, allowing them to make that connection. Instead they are bombarded by images of clothed animals speaking like humans, consequently they no longer accept them as a food source. When I was young, my friends and I played with horse shoes, rabbit tails and hens feet... the latter were great fun making the claws open and close!

We could view farm animals and envisage good food for the pot, so when the housewife's friends and neighbours realised that the home butchered meat was recognisable and oven ready, the orders started to come in, initially for a single joint but soon whole sides of pork were being ordered for the home freezer.

I had no difficulty in getting sales for my meat and proved that selling it 'oven ready' did bring in much more money per animal than selling them on the hoof, but there was a limit as to how many I could dispose of in that manner. The majority were sent to the market and still lost me money, but I did kill and butcher some myself and was quite proud of that achievement.

The first time I did the job myself, one of the local vets whom I knew well, called in at the piggery and dispatched the animal with his captive bolt humane killer. He then left and I spent the best part of the day doing what Frank had done in an hour, but I did end up with useable meat. I never did stun a pig or slit a sheep's throat... I would put the condemned animal in a pen with an earthen floor and shoot it in the head with my 0.22 rifle. That appeared to me to be the most humane way and I must admit that I found a great deal of satisfaction in being able to turn an animal into pot ready meat by my own hand.

However, satisfaction did not pay the bills and although I had earned a few extra pounds by home butchering, the basic problem still existed. My pig enterprise was losing money and I was reaching exhaustion.

CHAPTER TWELVE

(Going Under)

With the exception of those magical moments when I had the luxury of a few minutes sitting quietly beside a sow as she gave birth to beautiful little piglets or admiring a pen of well matched healthy pigs nearing market weight, the fourth year of my enterprise was not a happy time.

Even during the interludes as afore-mentioned, I was aware of the irony in the fact that the better my pigs performed, the more money I would lose, resulting in more worry being heaped on me.

Despite the efforts I had made to curb expenses and to increase returns, my overdraft remained stubbornly just below my limit. I had given my all and was now running on my reserve tank. For three years I had not one single day free of work and most days I had done the equivalent of two full time jobs.

I had rarely an outing lasting more than three hours with my wife and children. To use a vulgar modern expression, I had had no 'quality time' with Annette at all. I had missed out on birthday treats, Christmas celebrations and even relatives funerals. An evening by the fireside had been a rare treat, a full night's sleep a rarity and a holiday was totally out of the question.

My workload had not only been relentless but heavy and my wife only had to look at me to see the stress in my face and it was only when I saw the anguish in her face that I acknowledged that I was going under. Up until that point, she had kept her concerns to herself and had given me full support and encouragement with only minor caveats.

When I reflect on the workload that she too was bearing, raising a family of four on restricted income and without the physical support of her husband, I realised that she too must have been feeling the pressure. She admitted that the duress she was under was the pain of watching the man she loved working his fingers to the bone to achieve a goal and despite his blood, sweat and tears, failing in that mission.

To make matters worse, is ever such was possible, the bank manager began to pester me with phone calls demanding to know when I would be selling my pigs in order to reduce my overdraft? He did not even wait until I actually exceeded my limit, although I admit that it would have inevitably done so. I tried to explain the difficulties faced and how it would help if I could choose exactly when to market my stock, but it fell on very deaf ears.

He summoned me to his office and although I tried to explain the vagaries of the pig trade and why, if I took the pigs on to bacon weight, I may still not make a profit but would at least break even. His response was a blunt,

"No, sell what you can now."

That was the same individual who three years ago had shaken my hand and wished me well and as I walked from his office, I muttered to myself, "… and you Brutus."

I did as he instructed and sent every pig of marketable size to **Swans** and knocked several hundred pounds off the overdraft. I suppose that kept him happy, at least for the time being, but I began to feel even worse. I was having all the work and worry but was not in control. The writing was clearly on the wall.

Page 121

I could not see my situation improving and my tetchiness increased to the point where Annette pleaded with me to see our GP. However, a few more weeks of acrimony followed before I finally relented and made an appointment.

To tell the truth, by that time a morning off to visit the doctor was something to look forward to... in stark contrast, I was beginning to dread my visits to the piggery.

Doctors in those days were not restricted to five or ten minute per patient. He sat me down and I think that my gaunt appearance, shaky hands, trembling speech and tear filled eyes had already convinced him that I was in dire need... but not of medicine. He well knew of my domestic position but asked about my work to leisure balance and after telling him, he concluded that they were not just out of kilter but rather that the scales had fallen completely apart.

He found it incredulous that I could never have a day off and it was clear from his comments that he was worried about the effect is was having on my family, especially my dear wife. He prescribed sleeping pills but his advice was quite clear,

"You are doing two full-time jobs which has undoubtedly taken its toll. You will either have to give up the police or the pigs (ironically, some criminals would say that they were one and the same thing). You cannot carry on the way things are, so go home and seriously talk it over with your wife."

I did discuss things with Annette but knew only too well that there was only one solution. The choice was easy to make but difficult to accept. I would have to give up the piggery. The relief felt by Annette was palpable… just to hear me utter those words took a great weight off her shoulders as she knew that having agreed, I would not go back on my word. I think we even indulged in a little cuddle that night.

I still had several sows in pig and one or two with piglets at foot. All the store pigs had already gone on the instructions of the bank. There was no question now of an optimum time for marketing the remainder, I intended to just send them whenever they were big enough for the store ring and dispose of each sow as her litter was weaned.

Having worked out a timescale and the amount of feeding I would require to see it through, I was reduced to merely going through the motions… the sparkle, ambition, pride and optimism had all gone the way of my confidence. Things did pick up at home and because I was winding down, I was only doing the bare essentials at the piggery, allowing me a little more time domestically.

The children were bemused when I did not rise from the table and rush off. I remember the first time in over three years that I managed to attend a parents night at the school with my wife. That an ordinary event such as that could feel extraordinary, brought it home to me just how much I had denied myself and the family in the pursuit of my dream. But it was the little things which touched me most of all... being there at bedtime, watching the baby being bathed and having the time to listen to what had been happening at school that day.

As word spread that I was giving up the pigs, without exception, my friends and family agreed that it was the right thing to do. It was easy for them to say, they were not the failure!

Up at the piggery, things rolled along as usual and it did not take me long to muck out and feed as the numbers decreased. As each litter was weaned, the mother was dispatched off for hamburger meat... sows in some cases still in their prime or just past it. Those with still a lot to offer, were sent off for an early appointment with the slaughterhouse man because of Government ineptitude. It was not just tiny outfits like mine which were going to the wall, large well established herds were also being dispersed because of the unfair foreign competition.

The doctor had given me a choice over which of my jobs I should give up, but really, it was no choice at all. One was keeping us afloat while the other was determined to sink us... what kind of choice was that?

As luck would have it, the last sow to farrow was my particular favourite. I did not give any of them silly names, but I knew each one as an individual and this one was a particular character as well as being a very productive breeder. She had produced seven litters averaging nine pigs reared per litter, but it was also her friendliness which endeared her to me. She would often come up to me to have her ears scratched or her belly rubbed and was so very gentle with her piglets. She never showed any aggression when I handled her piglets… she was quite simply just a 'good un'.

I admit that I left her piglets with her beyond the eight week normal and even after they were weaned, I kept her a further few weeks, always being too busy to make the call to the market to book her in. I had time to spend with her, making her comfortable, making what little time she had left a pleasure for her. I always had a treat for her whenever I went to the piggery, some apples, stale bread or even just a divot I had pulled on my way to the holding. The ability or desire to butcher had deserted me.

In fact I kept her until her litter was big enough to go to market. I booked her in along with the young ones who would go on to some other farm to be fattened. Unless, and it was extremely unlikely, there was some other young man just starting out in pig breeding and who saw her potential, she unfortunately had a one way ticket to the abattoir. I tried to convince myself that she would be spared but in reality it was extremely unlikely.

I will never forget that morning when the lorry arrived to collect her and the last remaining store pigs. I had given them their breakfast and patted the sow as usual. She gulped down the food and stood looking at me with those trusting little eyes peeping out from below her lop ears. I had to walk away from her. I made ready the gates to guide them onto the lorry as I heard it rumble up the drive.

Fortunately it was one of the drivers I knew well and liked… it made it just a little bit less unpleasant handing her over to someone I knew who was never rough with the animals under his charge.

The store pigs made their usual squealing and attempting to thwart our efforts to load them, but as usual we came out on top. The sow on the other hand, just ambled onto the lorry and gave us no trouble at all, the most perfect beast to the last. As we closed the ramp behind them, I did not stop to exchange a few words with the driver, but walked back into the shed. I am sure he understood why and set off for the city with the very last of my dear pigs.

As I walked up and down the now empty piggery, my eyes filled with tears. I could not bring myself to clean out her pen. The brushes and shovels remained *in situ*, the feed barrow still half full, lay in the feed store, the unlit lamps dangled forlornly over the empty creeps and the weighing machine rested in the pen where it had been last used. It was desperately quiet. The life had literally gone out of the place.

I walked one last time the length of the piggery envisaging the pens once full of healthy, noisy pigs and I could swear I could hear the sows gently grunting to their piglets as I passed the farrowing crates. I slid the door closed and the thud echoed in the empty shed. Of course I did not actually cry, it was just the last remnants of dust stinging my eyes…

When I got home, there was no conversation with Annette, she just put her arms around me and said,

" No one could have done any more…"

However, given a level playing field, I honestly believe that I would have succeeded…

THE FINAL CHAPTER

(Winding Up)

It was a week or two before I could bring myself to return to the piggery after the departure of the last pigs. I do not suppose I would have gone had it not been for the fact that, even after selling off all my livestock, I still owed the bank slightly over £1,000. I had to sell up.

Had my application for planning permission to build a house on the holding been approved, I would have had no difficulty in selling the site to a developer and, without doubt, making a tidy profit? But it had been refused, as had a similar application in respect of **West Latch**. I did not have much luck when approaching **East Lothian Planning Department**, although it was within that same department, Annette was employed. It is interesting to note that there is a dwelling house on both those sites now, but at the time I had neither the money nor the will to pursue it further. I was in effect left with something which was practically unsaleable... who in their right mind wants a piggery when there is no money to be made in pigs?

When I went back to the firm of solicitors who had arranged the exchange from **West Latch** to **Hazyhill**, I learned to my horror just how unsaleable my property was... apparently it had no access from a public road!

Initially Hazyhill House, the piggery and the surrounding field had been in common ownership prior to being sold off in three separate lots. The crafty solicitors acting for the house purchaser had registered the boundary line between the house and the piggery as being along the centre of my access track, apparently to retain some influence over the activities of the piggery. They had registered the Title before those representing the purchasers of the piggery and the adjoining field, therefor their boundary stood.

My solicitor had not spotted this, hence I was left with a flawed Title. The only person I could sell the piggery to being the current owners of Hazyhill House... and they were only too well aware of the predicament I was in. They offered me 'sweets' for the piggery and I was in no position to refuse. It would appear that they subsequently obtained planning consent for the piggery and sold it at a substantial profit. The piggery and building have since been demolished and a lovely house now stands on the prime site... c'*est la vie*.

I was advised to sue my errant solicitors but I had neither the where with all nor the stomach for such a fight which I would probably have lost. It will be clear now as to why I did not identify the Firm of solicitors earlier and to be quite honest, I was just glad to walk away from the whole sorry episode.

I got enough money from the sale to pay off my bank overdraft with just enough left over to buy myself a smart shooting jacket I had long admired in **Mains the Saddlers**, Haddington.

I had lost £3000, worked countless hours of unpaid work, suffered a breakdown and forgone the more pleasant aspects of family life for... a new jacket! No wonder I treasured it.

Am I sorry I tried? Yes, but only because of Annette's tragic death just over a decade later. I regret having taken four years out of our marriage, but as well as proving not to have been a good businessman I could not see into the future. I did what I thought best at the time and failed, but at least I had tried. One thousand four hundred and sixty consecutive days without a break is no mean feat...

THE END

Printed in Great Britain
by Amazon

11073663R00082